Walking Through The Years

Walking Through The Years

Poetry For Life And Love

T. Craig Smith

authorHOUSE®

AuthorHouse™ LLC
1663 Liberty Drive
Bloomington, IN 47403
www.authorhouse.com
Phone: 1-800-839-8640

Published by AuthorHouse   01/23/2014

ISBN: 978-1-4918-5174-6 (sc)
ISBN: 978-1-4918-5173-9 (e)

Library of Congress Control Number: 2014901081

Any people depicted in stock imagery provided by Thinkstock are models, and such images are being used for illustrative purposes only. Certain stock imagery © Thinkstock.

This book is printed on acid-free paper.

This collection of Poetry is

dedicated to the memory

of Barbara Ann Gordon.

Introduction

Dear Reader,

Welcome to my world of Poetry. Over the last few years I've done a lot of introspective thinking. To put thoughts on paper I decided to use Poetry as a medium. I feel it is the most efficient way to describe what you are feeling in the most concise manner. I once attempted to write a novel, but it just didn't feel right.

Thanks so much for purchasing my book. I hope that you will find something in the following pages to identify with. If I can make you smile or perhaps evoke a single tear through my poems then I will consider my job done. Please keep on reading!

Sincerely,
Craig

I would like to thank the following people who each "played a part" in the creation of this book. They are as follows: Janet and Frank Gibbons, Fred and Barbara Gordon, Collette Hanson, Carol Hunt, Leslie Jacobs, Ruth Madigan, Jane McGibbeny, Ann Micheletti, Wendy Lee Perrero, Ellen Powers, Deb MacKenzie, Bobbi Sparks, Frank Walker, Randy Washington, Charles and Betty Weber, and Hank Ziegler.

Very special thanks go to my High School English teachers. Charles O'Malley and David Maier were instrumental in showing me the proper use of the English language, and how to express oneself in a beautiful way.

I would also like to thank Miss Cory Pawley who created the beautiful illustrations which are used to introduce both parts of this book. Cory is an aspiring young artist who desires someday to be a part of the burgeoning Video Game Industry. She wants to work in the development process from an artistic point of view.

The fantastic UFO photograph was taken by Mr. Richard C. Smith on a trip through Colorado in 2007.

The beauty of writing can be simply stated:

It has no future, it has no past;

It is always present

In the eyes and mind of the reader,

And it will forever last.

T.C.S.

Words For Life

"All the World's a stage,
And all the men and women merely players.
They have their exits and their entrances,
And one man in his time plays many parts,
His acts being seven ages."

Wm. Shakespeare

"Walking"

On the beach
Shuffling through the sand
Sticking to your feet
Like the bittersweet memories
Clinging to your mind;
The waves lapping at the shore
Like the blows you endured
For so many years.

Your tide can only get higher,
The lowest ebb already realized;
Set those sights on the future.
Shining skies could be just ahead;
Just put your best thoughts forward,
One at a time.
It can be as easy
As walking on the beach.

"Be My Compass"

Once you left
I lost my guiding light,
My Northern Star;
No wonder I have drifted afar
Since you disappeared from sight.

My careless feet have no direction,
No idea of where they're going
Or where they want to be.
My mind seems to wonder
To and fro,
Unable to focus, unable to grow.

It is said that no man is an island,
And perhaps it's true.
But for the lonely
It's like being surrounded
By an endless sea
When the mind like the water
Always seems blue.

Show me a sign, throw me a lifeline,
Rescue me from this despair;
I'm breathing the thinnest of air,
And drowning in the murkiest water.
My darkest thoughts
Are like Sharks encircling me.

Be my map, be my compass
In a world which appears
To have eluded my grasp;
A world I used to know,
But now seems so far away.

"Castles Of Sand"

From those tall parapets
It seemed like we could see forever.
Behind those strong walls
We could brave any storm;
The years have gradually eroded those beliefs,
And even the strongest
Can indeed come tumbling down.

The endless waves lap at that foundation
Weakening what we have built,
Exposing what we thought to be sacred.
They only strengthen with time
To become the storms
Which hasten the aging process
Along the way.

After all it's only sand,
And everything has its limits;
Those castles once so strong
Are almost gone now,
Mere bumps on the shore.
Those towers have fallen,
Those walls have floated away.
Even that insistent water
Threatens to flood the memory,
And wash well known things away.

There's nothing much left now;
At one time life felt so easy,
And should be easier the further we go,
But it's just not so.
All we can do is the final accounting,
Leave a message for future generations,
A few words of wisdom.

Build those walls up again.
Your tides will ebb and flow
As will the events in your lives
As they come and go.
You are the future architects
Of your very own
Castles in the sand.

"She Always Said No"

She seemed to be a happy girl,
But no one knew
That she held a secret
Nobody could be privy to.

The boys came by the score
Just for the chance
To knock on her door.
She would answer
In her own sweet way,
But always turned them all away.

During the Summer of her 25th year
She went far, far away.
Why? Her parents never would say.
No bags were packed to take along.
The only remaining question was when.

She had wanted love
Like any other girl,
But it was not meant to be;
Some have to live in tragedy,
And she always said no.

"Lost River People"

They're still among the missing,
Those familiar faces from long ago;
People we used to know,
But now no one knows
Where their lives have led.
Have we surrendered ourselves
By thinking them all left for dead?

We don't know exactly where they are
Or who they are these days.
For some inexplicable reasons
They remain in the dark.
It's like searching for a missing person;
Perhaps drowned by life's raging river,
That dark body of water
Which can overcome
Even the best of us.

Maybe they are lost forever,
Maybe it's their own silent way.
It could be for the best
That they don't come to the surface,
That we don't know them
For the people they have become;
So different from those
We thought we knew.

They're like lost river people,
Perhaps drowning in the depths
Of low esteem and self pity.
And they might never come back
To who they were.
Maybe it really is for the best
That dark water covers their faces
And hides their secrets,
And our memory of them
Has become a passing blur.

"Miss Fantasy"

She might be a beautiful blue eyed blonde,
Perhaps a fiery redhead,
She could even be that dark mystery,
But one thing is certain;
She is somebody's Miss Fantasy.

Every schoolboy's dream,
An older man's secret wish,
She's the stuff of legends made.
She might even be that girl next door.
Whatever it is she's got it,
And what it is
Will knock you to the floor.

She'll have that face
That could launch a thousand ships.
She could be anybody's Homecoming Queen.
Men will become fools
Just to be near her.
They will dream their senseless dreams,
And they will plot their crazy schemes.
But all those totally in vain.

That girl doesn't really exist;
It's why she has that name.
She is everything in our imagination,
That secret place where fantasy reigns.
But there's no harm in dreaming;
Just consider her part
Of one wonderful and never-ending game.

"Saucers Of Our Minds"

Humans have one thing in common,
Our endless curiosity;
Forever men have looked to the skies
Speculating about things they cannot see.
There have been so many theories,
But all unproven
When it comes to reality.

If Aliens do indeed exist
Perhaps they are searching
For the same answers
We always seem to be.
Maybe they do circle our world
As they watch our every move.
We probably appear to be Gladiators
As we scratch and fight for space
Almost every single day.

Maybe they don't explore at all.
Perhaps they live on some cold, distant planet
Watching and waiting for their visitors to arrive,
To lift them from their meagre lives
As compared to we.
But just maybe they survive in peace,
A concept mankind may never see.

Whoever they are,
Wherever they might be
Will probably remain the unanswered questions,
The eternal mysteries.
But they are always present in our minds
Like out of this world fantasies.

"Wasted Time"

Looking back on it now,
Giving it some serious thought
It sure felt like wasted time;
That desperate time I bought,
Those nights to be with you
Would only leave me bruised,
Thoroughly black and blue.

It was fun at the start,
But you weren't the type
Who could complement a lonely heart.
I knew you were headed for trouble,
And said goodbye just in time.

Life's lessons can be learned
In the hardest way;
Caution set aside and sobriety lost
You were the brew causing my stupor,
Bringing me down.
I was removed from character
And sacrificing ideals
At too high a cost.

A reckless need for attention
Can bring harm for company,
And it certainly blew my way.
You were the fruit feeding my ego,
You were the temptation I didn't need,
You were the girl out of time,
You were my Poetry
But not my rhyme.

"Nothing Good About Goodbye"

In the most awkward moment
It can be the hardest word to say,
A sad farewell for broken lovers
Who might never meet again,
Most assuredly not as friends.

So much has passed between,
Tons of emotion spent,
Ties that can never be quite broken,
Memories of their past together
Present in their minds forever.

In extreme it can witness
A most tragic ending:
Recall the story of Romeo and Juliet,
As cursed as two lovers could be;
Fooled by the illusion of death
He poisoned himself to join his beloved,
Or so he thought.
By the cruelest twist of fate
They lost their love eternally.

Despite not knowing
If another love will come their way
People are saying goodbye
Every second, every day,
But are left to question
If it's the proper word to say.

"Everything She Owns"

They can be seen almost anywhere;
Such lonely people,
So alone in their thoughts
Walking to nowhere,
No place to call home,
So very hard to watch,
Not as fortunate as you and I.

Everything she owns
In three brown paper bags,
All that remains of a former life;
Dragging them along
Barely clearing ground.
She once lived far, far away,
But got lost
Somewhere along the way.

Another day dawns like all the rest;
The weather just won't break.
She wanders through the sleet,
Through the rain
Clutching those bags,
Always the same.

As the rain became snow
She was last seen in the park
Spending the night on a bench
In the still of dark,
And there the following day,
Not moving but showing a frozen smile.
The bags open,
And in her hands the family photos
From a very long time ago.

"Carry Me Home"

People do need people;
Words that always ring true,
And if there's one thing I know
I can always depend on you.

You were always there
When I needed to talk,
Sort things out,
Point myself in the right direction
When it seemed like
I was walking in circles
With blinders on.

I've lost so much along the way;
Just how much hard to say.
But I've learned lessons
To never forget,
All well placed in my memory.

I almost felt lost at sea
Without faithful stars guiding me;
Out of nowhere you become my island,
And I could finally walk again
On your solid ground.

The missing pieces which were scattered
Now comfortably fit,
And I'm able to see straight ahead.
That light has turned green from red.
With your company I'm no longer alone;
Your help was all I ever needed
To carry me home.

"The Price"

She could be had for a price they say,
But it's much more than money you'll pay.
In your youth
You said you'd never give in,
And took a stand.
But too many lonely nights
Can alter the mind
Of even the strongest man.

In a moment of weakness
You make the call,
And she arrives by nine,
Lookin' oh so very fine.
Of course she shows you a good time,
But there's something missing,
Something you lost long ago.

The evening is short,
It's business as usual,
And she says a quick goodbye.
As she opens the door to go away
Something quietly passes by,
That lonely feeling,
That's the price,
The real price you have to pay.

"The Last To Know"

Funny thing about people,
They never tell you things
You need to know.
Last in line, last in respect
At times can have a devastating effect.

Words passed carelessly,
At times on purpose with cruel intent
Harm us when we least expect.
Those moments can be world changing,
Love life rearranging.
The people involved, it always seems,
The last to know.

Love's arrows can be sublime,
But the poison darts we have to watch;
Stories passed on by a third,
By someone with no respect
For the parties involved.
No ultimate responsibility
For those words spoken
About husbands and wives,
Threatening to ruin their lives.

And how many times
Did you know of a secret lover,
A person who longed for you?
Others seemed to suspect,
Maybe some even knew.
But it passed without culmination,
Lost in someone's sleepy memory.
As always you were the last to know.

"Only Numbers"

Days are really only numbers,
In youth as high as you could count,
As far ahead as you could see;
There was no limit
As to who you could be.

As we age the numbers become compressed,
Starting to tighten the noose.
With time and numbers
We are too obsessed,
And we can't seem to stay loose.

Now all the Math is finally done,
We've reached our common goal.
The final accounting has taken its toll.
Our lives are recounted on stones of grey
Standing in fields of green.
But what does it all really mean?

The numbers no longer mean a thing,
No longer do they rule our lives,
No longer make us question or wonder.
Only one remains with true meaning;
It's that we're all together,
Six feet under.

"Land Of Cotton Candy"

Remembering those days
When clouds looked like Cotton Candy;
Those times so clear and shiny,
Whatever you imagined or wanted to see,
Happily viewed in illusory ways.

A child's days were carefree and bright,
Everything seemed so right;
No worries, no responsibility,
The gift of youth, a placid serenity.

As we age our seasons change;
Summer shortens as does Spring.
We enter the Autumn of our lives,
And not nearly as often
Do we dance and sing.

We begin the Winter of our time,
Perhaps one last fling.
Our days become clouded with harsher weather.
We're almost on opposite ends of the globe,
Only a sliver of fading light
As compared to a strobe.

Our lives change so with time,
Distantly removed from our prime.
That Cotton Candy is not nearly as soft;
It now gives one stickier fingers,
And can be so much harder to wash off.

"Lost Southern Way"

Your fields of green still stand strong,
Your mountains still smoky,
Echoing that same old Dixie song,
But something is very wrong;
Your boys are not coming home.

Those fields have also run bloody red;
Terrible things were done and said.
Your sons farmed those fields,
Fished those streams,
Courted their girls, had their dreams.
It seems like they never left,
It just seems.

That was a long time ago.
There are those who still say
It was never meant to be,
And there are those
Who still stop to cry and grieve.

Some believe that spirits still walk those fields,
And they still wear the Chestnut and Gray,
Proudly waving their flags,
Rebels with a cause.
Those boys fought for their way of life,
The Yankees with not as much to say.
It all makes you pause to wonder;
What if the War had gone
The Southern way?

"The Other Side Of The Mountain"

The air always damp and still,
And ever present that disturbing chill.
The climate complete with clouds and rain,
But it's the fog, that surrounding shroud
That so confuses my thinking.
Lost in this maze without direction,
So frightening at times
I've felt like screaming out loud.

For what seems like years
I have held residence there;
Unlike a home,
More like a Wolf's lair.
Stuck deep in the bowels
Of desperation and incoherency,
Often feeling like the beast
That should be living there.

This side of the mountain
No longer has a place for me.
Like the weight of its boulders
Inexorably it holds me down,
Feeling my face only a frown,
Never a smile, no laughter to be found.
Despite the crags and niches
I begin my climb,
That of the most challenging kind.

The higher I progress
Smoother is the terrain,
Left behind those clouds and rain.
I feel lighter now
As the murkiness departs my brain.
Continuing the arduous journey back

To Life, to the other side,
So many thoughts course through my mind.
It had seemed like a nightmare, not real,
Those wasted hours, those empty days
Spent in scary isolation
When nothing seemed to matter.

As I reach the pinnacle
Knowing my time had come,
The moment to shed the Wolf's clothing,
That melancholy feeling,
Breaking free from the chains
Which had imprisoned me,
Ready to lose the past and look ahead,
The warm Sun lighting the way.

Like an old friend with a helping hand
A whole new world shows its face.
It is as I remembered,
But it's been so many years
Since I had left.
There is much to rectify,
And it's about time
To erase all my fears.

"Night Fliers"

We fly while others walk,
We are wakeful while others sleep,
We are creative while others merely talk,
Our minds scale literary mountains steep.

Some would say that we are only ghosts
Just quietly slipping by,
Our human bodies just temporary hosts
To our souls and spirits reaching high.

To write about things we love,
No thoughts barred, no words forbidden;
This human life we strive to rise above,
Constantly in search of meanings hidden.

It's no surprise that sleep comes hard
To those who dream and visualize,
To those whose emotions have played a card,
To those who wear no makeup, no disguise.

There are those who feel our joy,
And at times those who feel our pain.
We see things others don't,
And we write them down when others won't.
We are the writers,
We are the lonely fliers,
Creatures of the night.

"La Escena" (The Stage)

Twisting the red with flair
He is the peoples' hero,
El Matador.
Lives his life on a dare,
He and the Bull meet at point zero;
They meet on the killing floor.

Approaching one another,
One with calm precision,
The other rude with anger.
The air is still,
The crowd anticipating
The Bull rush to come
The blood to be let.

One pass, then another,
El Matador like a magician
Stepping like a Flamenco dancer,
The Banderillas striking
With deadly precision.
The beast now weakened,
But also strengthened with rage
Will take a last bow
On this bloody stage.

The Plaza De Toros falls silent,
The people fixated on their hero.
The finish is now beckoning
As the two face the reckoning.
The Black is on his knees
As El Matador closes with ease.

The bloody sand will be stained again
As in Old Spain of centuries past.
And as those violent memories last
We think of the man with skill,
The perpetrator of the kill.
But our ultimate hero?
The one who gave his life,
El Toro.

"A Final TKO"

I was there when it all began,
Your wonderful White Wedding Day.
If I had only known
I would have had my say;
You would have turned
And ran away.

Sometimes we don't know
What's in store,
What the other side is thinking,
What makes them crash
Through that bedroom door,
What makes them love less,
Not more.

I read about you last night;
Your life story was all there
In somber black and white.
You finally gave up that fight,
And I was powerless to help you.
They found you lying face down
All wrapped in Black and Blue.

"My Rasputin"

You've seen the dark side of life,
But always managed to leave it behind,
Unscathed and guilt free
While others were caught in the undertow
Falling victim to your misdeeds
And your egocentric greed.

You had me for a little while,
Right where you wanted me to be
Until I discovered who you really were;
You were that hint,
That dirty little secret
Whispered in my ear,
That tap on my shoulder
I shouldn't have paid attention to,
That clever suggestion
To get involved in sin
Before I knew what I was in.

Like a blood sucker in the night
Searching for its next helpless victim
Your lust knows no bounds.
It's almost as if you have nine lives,
Immune to silver bullets
And the poisoned arrows
Aimed at your heart.
Those are good things for your kind,
Because you thrive on the ignorance
Of those poor souls who would be blind.

The smart ones among us
Have figured you out by now;
We know how to deal
With your self serving mind,
Always putting yourself first,
Drinking in all the pleasure you can handle,
No matter the cost to those around you.

We realize that you will never die out,
Your kind will always be here.
But the key to our survival
Is to ignore your plea for attention
And your constant cry for pity.
From us you will get nothing,
No help,
Not even the slightest tear.

"We Forgot"

For the longest time
We were the best of lovers.
But it seems so very long ago
Since your lips last touched mine.
Somehow we lost all feeling,
No longer could we sing along.

Our mountains became too tall to climb,
Our rivers too wide to swim,
We felt less together
And more out than in.
We both harbored secrets,
And forgot what it was like
To be the best of friends.

People can change and usually will.
We didn't recognize the danger signs
While slowly slipping away was our mutual thrill.
Our blue skies became a cloudy grey.
We couldn't forgive,
And lacked the proper words to say.

Looking back to those halcyon days
It's still tough to figure;
How we got lost in that unforgiving maze,
Speaking with the strangest tongues,
Walking in the most disoriented ways.
Our world once held together
With the strongest glue
Tragically gave way, split in two.
Too afraid to question why,
But we knew.

"Just Too Sexy"

Across the dance floor with ease
She slides like the ultimate tease.
Oozing with life and personality,
Being sexy is her only priority.

Dancing hot is just her thing;
This chick has all the moves.
Knowing exactly what she's doing
She ain't into fooling,
But she is into those dancing grooves.

Watching her can make you sweat,
She should be against the law.
She'll shackle you with invisible cuffs,
And you're helpless to move
When she's in that kind of mood.

This kind of girl is trouble,
She moves like no woman should,
Too sexy for her own good.
Men who watch become wreckage,
Mere rubble in her sensual wake.

But here's the rub, the final word:
She'll meet her match as everyone does;
A clever Casanova will sweep her off her feet,
See through her sexual facade
Without skipping a beat.
He'll wink and give that knowing nod
As if to say
That she's just a woman.
We wouldn't have it any other way.

"Honey For Sale"

As long as money and sex rule the world
There will be an available girl;
The three intertwine like branches on a tree
That will never die.
Like Apples bright and red
They just keep hanging around,
But their taste is mostly bittersweet.

They can come in all colors,
And can smell like irresistible nectar.
Black, white, yellow, and shades in between,
But the only color they know is green.
They won't remind anyone of that special girl,
That Homecoming Queen.
If that time could always be now,
But it was a very long time ago.

One short hour of deluded glory
Can't erase the memory
Of so many lonely nights
Or dispassionate days ahead;
It's just a small part
Of a sad, continuing story.

Be careful not to fall too far
Into that endless, bottomless pit.
Don't get too used to that forbidden taste
And the jaded side of your mind.
The beauty of life
Doesn't get paid by the hour.
And always remember that anything sweet
Can always turn sour.

"The Abyss"

As you look into that bottle
The empowering liquid now gone,
And so everything has a beginning
And has an end.
Same as with life,
But your time is closing every day,
And you can't have it back.

It doesn't matter how rich you are.
It won't help you now.
Bits of you are breaking away
From what was your whole.
Look at that pretty face in the mirror.
In a few precious years only a memory,
You may not be here at all.

Inside that bottle,
A slippery place to be,
Inside that bottomless pit
Thinking that your safety
Is the pretty color within,
But its only way is losing,
Never to win.

If you would only cry,
Let yourself go,
Exorcise those spirits holding you so.
You might start scaling those walls of glass
To start the long journey back,
The toughest test of your life.

It's time to grow up now,
Escape the world of self doubt and pity,
Low self esteem.
You have a new person to be,
Your new world can shine for you.
Open those eyes and you'll see.

"Old Hippies Never Die"

His hair once so dark
Swept into a ponytail now
In a subtle shade of grey.
The body not quite the same,
But the mind still there
When hopes were high,
And the sweet smell of Pot
Made pungent the air.

The old records and music
Take him back
To the time of his life
And those young love affairs;
They were free and always there.
And the concerts and the chicks
Asking for spayre chaynge.
He smiles to himself
Recalling those peaceful days.

He remembers how flowers once adorned hair,
When the peace sign was a way of greeting,
How girls forgot their Bras and didn't care.
It's not hard to see
Why those times were the best
With little care and less responsibility.

When I see one of those guys now
I can't help but grin.
I may not look the part,
But I remember as well.
Those memories burn deep
Within my heart,
That freak flag still flies high,
And we old Hippies never die.

"Like Painted Ladies"

They come in all shapes and sizes
Replete with color and noise,
Their faces well painted
For all the foolish boys;
Their pretty looks beckon
And lure you in
If you don't mind
Your pockets becoming awfully thin.

Like painted ladies all in a row
They tease you to play
Knowing that sooner or later
You'll succumb to their shiny glow.
Deep inside you know it's a losing game,
But you'll place your bets
All the same.

They're not worth the investment made,
All the money you paid.
There are those who always smile,
Who count the profits coming in
For the times you played and lost,
And laugh walking to the bank
All the while.

They're only machines after all,
But the real ladies can be just as cold
In their own special way,
Not interested in what you have to say.
But the temptation for both is strong;
Your desire to play
Can only be ignored for so long.

Take the chance if you will,
But know this for sure:
They will become little more
Than an expensive and most transient thrill.

"La Pobrecita" (the poor little one)
The story of Eva Duarte Peron

A rag to riches story
If there ever was one.
Your light burned so bright,
But only for the shortest time,
Your rise to fame like legends made.

Just a poor country girl from the start,
But there was wanderlust in your heart.
You went to the city with great ambition,
And it didn't take long
To discover what had to be done,
How to play your part.

Sleeping your way to the top,
Such an overused cliché,
But all the right doors were opened
When you were willing to give
What men do and always want.
It was only a matter of time
When everything you ever desired
Arrived in your fleeting prime.

You smiled at all the right people,
And married the most powerful man,
But had your critics along the way.
In the common peoples' hearts
You were always number one,
Could do no wrong.
But who could know that a deadly disease
Was about to hasten your Swan Song?

All your beauty and power
Were not enough in the end.
Your glow faded away
At such an early age;
At 33 La Pobrecita, beloved Evita
Had turned her very last page.

"Satyrical Mind"

A figment of your imagination,
The terror of your dreams,
But he can be so real.
Like a serial stalker
Pretending to be
An everyday park walker.

He can simulate being your friend,
He could be the nice young man next door.
But when you allow him into your world
He can turn it upside down.
The plain and simple fact is
That he is everywhere
In each and every town.

He might be a man of leisure
Or a man who works hard labor,
But the two have one thing in common;
It's something they savor,
And sooner or later
They'll play that trump card
To win your highly guarded treasure.

With their persuasive charm
They can bring you to the floor.
They can wow you with money,
But be well warned
Each and every Honey;
Eventually you'll be mistreated
Like the average whore.

So he can be a man of many faces
Hiding in your mind's darkest spaces.
If all this sounds real creepy,
A bit too scary
Just look up "Satyr" in your dictionary.
He's real fact, not at all fictionary.

A man of lechery and lust
Should be fair warning to all maidens;
Venture forth if you must,
But be very, very careful
With whom you place your trust.

"Two Different People"

Nights when I'm all alone
My thoughts turn to you,
And how far away you are
And how empty is my heart.
My hopes have all turned cold
As if cast in stone.
I'll never forget the day
Our love fell apart.

What you are now
And what you were then,
Two different people,
Hardly the girl I used to know.
You've made me feel
Like a useless has been.

Our love once so wide and deep
Seems so dried up now,
Mountains easy to climb
Appear way too steep.
It's funny how time changes things
And the feeling a lost love forever brings.

If our paths ever again cross
We might not recognize
The two before our own eyes.
Too much pain
Can cloud the mind
Which wants to recall
The better time
Not the bitter cost.

"Not So Original Sin"

Two souls searching for a spark
Under the guise of love;
A chance meeting,
A dingy roadside bar
With sad country songs
Providing the background,
Giving her the excuse for tears,
And that broad shoulder to lean on.

Out on the town looking for something
Not really there,
Certainly not worth
Throwing twenty years away;
Leaving their rings behind,
Their married promises as well,
Hoping for a second Heaven
When all they might find
Could be like Hell.

Some may think it's fun,
Others might say it's just a game,
But without love
It can never be the same.
A few short hours of misdirected passion
With only losers playing,
And the bitter aftertaste, that empty feeling
Only serves to leave
The guilty cheaters reeling.

No words can soften what they've done
In places they should have never been.
Like shooting stars on a collision course
They never had a chance,
And what remains for both
Sure feels like sin.

"Queen Of Hearts"

That girl is such a mystery,
So many things you can't see;
Two people rolled into one,
She's got you fooled and then some.

She dances around you
With steps you've never seen;
You can't lead nor can you follow
What she seems to be.

She'll show you the best of times
And the worst as well.
You're only fooling yourself
To be expecting much more.

You can give her
All the dollars you have,
But it makes no sense;
All you're left with is nothing
Save cruel recompense.

Like the clever magician
Whose tricks you can never quite figure
She'll lay her cards on the table.
It's up to you to choose,
But beware when you enter her game,
Because this Queen of Hearts
Can make a joker out of you.

"Letting The Fantasy Go"

It hurts to tell you no;
Real circumstance makes it so.
In a distant space and time,
No doubt,
I would have made you mine.

We must go our separate ways.
You have the gift of youth;
I've seen my better days.
The best times for you
Can only be straight ahead.

As a younger man
I would pursue you endlessly;
You would never escape.
Call me a stalker if you must,
But all I desire for now
Is to see you safe,
And to have your trust.

Our precious time together well spent,
But so quickly almost gone,
Languishing as if only a fading dream.
I'll always wonder
What it all meant;
Fantasy to reality and back
It might well seem.

I'll be gone long before you realize
What we've given to one another's lives.
So please remember me
As the lucky one
Who will forever cherish our time,
And always remember you.

"The Actress"

When I first noticed you
Your world was a stage,
Your lines well rehearsed,
Your act all the rage.
I watched you up close and from afar.
You had all the makings of a superstar.

But I no longer recognize the face,
The girl I used to know;
You've become a wanderer
From place to place.
The hard life you live
Is starting to show.

I was your leading man
And you my lady,
But the plot was always confusing,
Our lines so hazy.
Troubles have swept your winning smile away,
And drugs have pulled you down.
When I see you now
There is good cause to frown.

It appears that greed
Has spoiled the plot;
It's all about the money you want,
And the money I haven't got.
The line is drawn
Between you and me;
The real girl
I've now begun to see.

The audience was poised for the final act,
But you failed to show.
Your makeup has worn all too thin,
The photos don't lie;
It's all there in black and white,
And what I'm seeing
Is no pretty sight;
You have the look of a real pro.

"The Girl From Yesterday"

Remembering you like it was yesterday,
Standing in front of me
Looking as good as you could be.
A girl hard to match,
There had to be a catch,
Something I didn't quite see.

Those moments I stole from time
To be in your life
Were like a beautiful dream,
A romantic fantasy.
And wondering if it could be real,
If we could ever be.

We had times I'll cherish forever,
Some of the best I'd ever known.
But when the seeds of reality started to grow
It reminded me
Of what I really didn't want to know,
That you were much younger,
And my age was starting to show.

I always felt we were dancing around
On some imaginary stage,
Our script too good to be believed,
You making me feel half my age.
In reality my years remaining few,
And then I realized
What our audience already knew,
That stories don't always have
The happiest of endings.

As the years pass by,
And my memories start to fade
One will stay constant and true,
Of the night you said goodbye to me.
You were never really gone,
You were just the girl who couldn't be.

"Looking The Other Way"

Thought I saw you yesterday;
Maybe my mind was playing
Its usual tricks on me.
It had been so long
Since we had said a sad goodbye.
I was convinced
You were forever gone.

But that walk turned my head,
Sultry moves I had seen before;
It reminded me of someone
I had known.
The forced smile so familiar,
That unmistakable look on your face,
Trying so very hard
Not to acknowledge me.

I thought of waving
But shut it down;
Knowing what is lost
Is best forgotten.
Sometimes you can't return
To where you were,
The good times of a past affair.
Just remember the best
And let it stay.
So I kept on walking
And looked the other way.

"Dark Obsession"

Obsession: The act of an evil spirit in possessing or ruling a person.

To enter your world risky at best,
Into a web of sticky lies;
It was my ultimate test,
Just maybe my final rest.
The Spider's way is to devour her mate,
To nourish her all consuming hunger;
Perhaps you've been plotting my demise.

Lured by seductive tricks
My mind cannot wish you away
Nor can I wash my dirty hands.
You haunt me in my dreams
As I see your face,
Broken now it seems.
It's been so very long
I can no longer put the parts together
To paint your fading entity.

But now that you obsess my very soul
I desire your every inch,
I want to breathe your breath
As if it was mine.
To lay by your side night and day,
To be your private clothing,
To feel the erotic nature of your skin,
To be inside your mind,
To know what resides within,
To be that close,
My ultimate fantasy.

I've stalked you for miles and miles,
Been everywhere I thought you'd be.
It's almost as if you're a ghost
Vanishing from my life
When I want to see.
Changing roles is my final plan,
And this time around
I'll be holding the key.

At my long journey's end
I will find you, to hold you,
And to love you once again.
Finally my feet will find the floor,
And you will be knocking once more
Upon my lonely door.

"Trace Of Red"

Only the smallest mark remains now,
Not equal to the bruising on my heart.
Your memory still lingers somehow,
But is fading fast
Like that trace of Red.

I remember your lips,
Oh so very well,
Graced with the color
I see every day.
I recall the warmth
As your mouth melted mine.
But even then you gave me a sign
As clouds replaced the sunshine.

We went a little too fast
As time between us passed.
Instead of black and white
We seemed to be a shade of grey.
I never did have the final say.

At times I feel older now,
But as I see that trace
Youth again becomes familiar to me.
And as my memory repaints your lovely face
It also recalls a love,
Perhaps not meant to be.

You left that mark
The last night together,
Perhaps a sign, a calling card;
I'll never quite know,
But it's been awfully hard.
At least the Sun rises every day,
And that trace of Red
Is finally fading away.

"Every Time It Rings"

Only one matters these days,
But it doesn't come to me;
Not the call I really want,
The one I'd cancel all others to receive.

If I could only hear your voice
It would renew my faith
In love I thought to be lost,
In trust I thought to be gone.
Silence is piercing my heart now
As I sink to the floor
Clutching that phone.

Every time it rings
I imagine you're there,
But it seems you are gone forever,
Having faded from sight,
Never to shed any light
On why or where.

So every time it rings
I jump to attention
Only to be let down again,
To curse my fate.
I know that someday
That call will be there,
On the other end your voice,
But maybe a little too late.

"Falling"

Falling into you,
Deep into you
Was like being high
On a powerful drug.
It was like flying high
Through a meteor shower
Blinded by your light.
But things weren't
What they seemed to be,
And you weren't the girl
I thought to be free.

You told lies,
Always wore a disguise,
Afraid to love yourself,
And it showed in the worst of ways.
Deceit can return to haunt,
And you won't like how it repays.
I remember your eyes;
They never looked straight at me,
Always furtive, side to side.
It told me loads about your mentality.

You were afraid to enter
The world of normalcy,
Always played the part
Of the downtrodden girl.
You were what
Others thought you should be,
Too scared to walk
Your own way.

You were falling into
That neverending chasm,
The one of semi-sanity
Dragging me with you
Along the way.
But I broke free
From the way you wanted me to be,
And I left you,
Falling hopelessly.

"Like A Category 5"

The flags were flying,
All the signs were there,
But he chose to ignore them.
He never knew what hit him
When she arrived like a Category 5,
The damage done still easy to see.

If he had only known
It could have been different.
But he needed somebody to hold,
And she gave him
What he had forgotten
A long time ago.

She felt so right
In all the ways he wanted,
But he didn't listen
To what she was really saying;
That body language,
The obvious he never paid attention to.

Blown away by a pretty smile
And a sexy way,
In reality a thin facade
Masking all the trouble she was into.
Despite the signs of stormy weather
He set sail anyway.

Now all he has are bittersweet memories
As he tries to reclaim his life,
The way he used to be.
He can only shake his head
Thinking of those worrisome days,
But at least he's finally free.

"There's Always One"

There's always one
Who will drive you out of your mind,
And she could be a woman
Who might be the most troubling kind.
You cling to every word she says,
And are seduced
By every move she makes.
But she'll leave you hanging on
Just when you thought
She might be the one.

There's always one
Who will rob you blind,
And make a fool of you.
She'll bring you down
When you were as high
As you could be.
You'll follow her anywhere
Despite knowing
She's laid your emotions bare.

When you really need her
She won't be there;
You'll be grasping at straws,
Nothing more than desperate air.
As she walks away
She'll be smiling all the while
Knowing that around the bend
There's always one,
Another victim to be had.
You just never realized
Any woman could be that bad,
But there's always one.

"A Game For Fools"

It's a game played by fools,
And it's all you ever do;
It appears I'm ever your pawn
In a continuing story
Where it seems the curtain
Will never be drawn.

Mysterious phone calls
Late at night,
No message, no voice
On the other end.
If I had the choice
My wish would leave only you,
That you are still reaching out,
Trying to somehow get through.

I no longer have a bluff,
It's your call;
The next move belongs to you.
You've always had the better hand,
And I'm the one who's gambling
With my heart on the line.

I feel so dizzy these days
Like being caught on a wheel of Roulette;
My mind like the ball,
Endlessly spinning 'round,
Not sure of my final fate;
Maybe now it's just too late,
Maybe we've sung our final song,
And the love I had bet on,
Finally gone.

"In Focus Now"

Saying goodbye to you,
One of the hardest things I'll ever do.
Like falling stars in a midnight sky
We burned the brightest,
But only for the shortest time.
From different worlds
You had your way, I had mine,
But it was still worth the try.

You were my Eve in the Garden of Eden,
But like the serpent
You came with sticky tongue
And the sweetest of lies.
Taken by your beauty and a chance for fun
I almost fell too deep
Before I realized
What was happening before my eyes.

We had met in the darkest of places
Where men try to heal their lonely lives.
My fall should have been no surprise;
I was the one out of control.
For me it had become a matter of the heart;
You were only playing your accustomed part.

So perhaps it's best that it ended
Before the truth got too twisted and bent
You gave me what I needed to be sure;
For the heartbroken you were the cure,
But I finally began to see
That your attention wasn't only for me.

If we ever meet again
I'll remember fondly what happened then.
At times you have haunted me
Like a spirit from the past,
But it was a one sided love
That could never last.

"The Fallen"

You had your moments,
You stood out from the crowd.
What happened in between
I will never quite know.
Suffice it to say
You've moved on to a distant place
Where you've become a stranger now.

Those lines under your eyes
Where once rested smiles
Explain a lot of your story;
They show hard times
Not the brief flirtation with glory.
You nearly had it all
When you were standing tall.
It was nothing more than a sham,
All window dressing
For one weak and lonely man.

You came to me
When my spirit was dying,
And my heart was bleeding out.
You gave me what I needed,
What only you could give.
If I could only repay you now
I would give my thanks,
But more importantly,
Bring back the girl I knew
From a happier day.

I can only smile these days
When I recall those beautiful nights
We spent together
Which now seem so very distant.
As I look at your photos now
They return to life,
Albeit for the briefest moment
The girl I had hoped you could be.

"Walking Through The Years"

It all starts with baby steps
Which get larger as you go,
And before you realize what's happening
You're walking through the years.

Time seems so fleeting,
And you wonder where it goes;
Before you know it your time has come,
And hard to believe
When it's almost over and done.

Walk with giant steps while you're here;
You only have so long
To leave a lasting impression,
To make your mark,
And to pacify your wandering mind.

Live this life with grace,
Help others when you can,
Keep your ideals through thick and thin,
And learn from everything
You're involved in.

Hope for only the best,
More smiles than tears,
More courage than fears
As you go walking through the years.

"Slowly But Surely"

If you're careful with it,
Not rush and take it slow
No reason you can't have it all,
The way you were
Before the crazy started.

It's been more than long
Since the darkness closed your eyes.
At times you felt disguised
Wearing the cloth of another man,
That clothing clearly undersized.

Silence your partner way too long,
But became deafening to your ears.
The cacophony confused days with years
As the hours crawled slowly by,
And the quicksand pulled you down.

How it all started difficult to figure,
The way out harder to visualize,
But focus on what you enjoy.
You'll feel like yourself again.
Slowly but surely,
The life you love will come.

"For No Bloody Reason"

"It is well that war is so terrible. We shouldn't grow too fond of it."
Robert E. Lee

It's Hell on Earth
To those closely involved,
But it touches the lives
Of so many more.
Man versus Man,
We call it war.

Down through the ages
We just can't quit,
Can't love our neighbors enough
To stop taking lives.
At times it feels like pure survival,
The spoils going to only the tough.

Generals calling upon men
To commit horrible acts,
Those seen in the worst of times,
To spare no citizen,
Even women and children in harm's way;
Everyone is caught in the fray.

The reasons can be simple or complex;
The desire for land,
A thirst for riches,
Even that subtle sin, Jealousy.
Some fight in aggression,
Some merely in self defense,
But the results all too familiar
As blood once again soaks sand.

Conflict always seems in season,
But men still question,
Wondering who the actual leaders are;
Maybe those behind closed doors
Making all those dark decisions,
Sometimes for no bloody reason.

"The Beanstalk"

Some men seek riches
Beyond their wildest dreams.
Others are satisfied with notoriety,
A chance to be recognized
Above all others
For what they have the vision to see.

Some thrive with thrills and danger
While others are happy with Poetry and Prose.
Fortunate are they who have both,
Opportunity to do all things
Before their lives close.

The journey can be fraught with danger,
Problems along the way;
There are mountains to scale,
Ladders to climb,
Some even have their giants to slay.
Some die attempting to get there,
Victims of their own special greed.
Some know to keep things under control
As they progress and quietly succeed.

With the passing of each and every day
A man will start seeing the light,
Get closer to a job well done.
But there are pros and cons
For as long as a man will live;
He must learn to handle both,
Whatever his life is meant to give.

"Literal Addiction"

Why I keep writing I just don't know.
I want it fast, never slow.
It's fact, no longer fiction;
I'm introducing my new addiction.

Words flow from heart and head
So fast I can't even keep track.
There's no peace in going to bed;
Even late at night there's no slack.

In my youth I dreamed of such,
But with it I never did much.
Now with a breaking heart
I've started playing the writer's part.

Ideas come from what I see and hear,
And from what I already know.
People and Love seem to come first,
Nature and History not far behind,
All attempting to satisfy my thirst.

I don't want this feeling to end,
And my best could be just ahead.
Bear with me anyone I call friend
For a different me and more
Is just around the bend.

Words For Love

"What is love? Tis not hereafter;
Present mirth hath present laughter;
What's to come is still unsure;
In delay there lies no plenty;
Then come kiss me, sweet and twenty!
Youth's a stuff will not endure."

Wm. Shakespeare

"A Chance In Time" (Bobbi's Poem)

We will never be here again
As time stands still;
Our chance for a lasting memory
If I ask and you will.

What brought us together
We may never know,
But it's fair to say
I want you more every day,
And your yes will make it so.

Born in different times
But of common heart and mind,
A man and woman seeking love,
Perhaps their last chance of all.

So look into my eyes
To see my soul,
And hold me with all your strength.
Take full advantage of what I'm giving,
Do not cast good fortune away.

Lay with me now
To give me hope
That we may combine two halves
To form an everlasting whole.

"Love Once Lost"

Today you gave me the news
I never wanted to hear;
Those words so calmly stated,
You never shed a tear.

Your time is short
I know that now.
I'll be missing a love
I might have never had anyhow.
Perhaps it's for the best;
Losing you that way
Would be the cruelest test.

In another life we'll meet again;
I can feel it somehow.
And l'll hold you tight,
You'll never get away.
My words will sound so right,
My dreams will all come true,
And a love once lost
Will never again go astray.

"Forty Too Late"

We met much too late,
Dealt the cruelest blow
By crazy fate.
Two souls with much in common,
But generations keeping us apart.

Good things can happen
When two people listen,
And keep an open mind.
We might just get together
If one is willing,
And the other agrees
Not to be blind.

What you'll see is a man
Willing to sacrifice,
Impart a little knowledge and good advice,
But above all
Treat you with respect,
And appreciate you so much more.
Your feelings will never become
Victims of neglect.

What you will afford me
Is the Fountain of Youth,
A chance to breathe fresh air again,
A second coming if you will,
A new life with you until.

Years down the road
When I'm dead and gone
You'll be sadly asking yourself
About how fast the time went.
Funny, 'cause I was thinking the same
When I first laid eyes on you.

"Traces To Remember"

If I stare at those old photos too long,
If I listen to that familiar song
They bring back the places,
They put together those traces
Of what we used to be
When I was into you,
And you were into me.

The crumpled tickets from our first date,
That feeling when I first saw you,
It still flows.
Your lock of hair,
It still lives in my wallet,
The plant you left,
It still grows.

I wondered for years
Where you had gone,
Where you had decided to fly,
Why you gave no reason why.
Only these traces remain
To remember you by.

"Sweet Torture"

Loving a man in totality
At times ignores reality.
Knowing him for what he really might be,
The most difficult task.

The strings of her heart
Controlled by a man with none;
He plays with her like a puppet,
Whatever his desire or whim.
Strangely she craves it,
But it's really no longer fun.

Sad to see a woman hanging on,
True love eluding her grasp.
She cries about the way they were;
Now it's no more than a blur.

Perhaps a stranger could bring her back.
He could join the fight,
And show her a clearer light,
Of how her life could really be.

If he only had a chance
She might learn what real love is,
What it should be.
He could be the dam to stop her tears,
To soothe her feelings, calm her fears.

Her lost love has been shattered like glass
In so many pieces.
But like a puzzle with scattered parts
It can be solved
By the fusion of two willing hearts.

"One In A Thousand"

If I say it a thousand times
It will never be enough
To say what I'm feeling,
To say what you already knew,
That I'm truly in love with you.

If I could be with a thousand girls
I would turn them all away,
To be with only one.
Once again you already knew
That one in a thousand would be you.

If I could hear a thousand names
I would remember only one.
That's the way I want it to be
As we live our lives together,
You and me.

If I had to do it all again,
Maybe a thousand times
It wouldn't be necessary,
Because you're everything I needed;
After the first time I knew.

If I could pray a thousand prayers
Only one needs to be listened to,
That you would be mine forever,
My one in a thousand,
Because I'm truly in love with you.

"Just One Kiss"

Surrealism: The interpretation of the workings of the subconscious mind as manifested in dreams.

It may seem the simplest of things,
But just one kiss,
A tender and sweet caress
Means all the world
As I enter the Autumn years
With little hope of Spring ahead.
As the finality steadily nears
It's what I'll sorely miss.

As I hold you closely now,
Perhaps for the final time,
Scenes of my life
Rushing through my mind,
My desire to make this moment
Last forever.
If we only have one life to live,
One pass to make it through
Then this is the one memory
Hardest to surrender
About you.

The softness of your touch
Can never be replaced,
That smile looking down upon me,
The curve of your mouth
Which I've traced a thousand times
In my sleep, in my dreams,
And in my reality.
I'll remember all these parts of you,
And more
As the feeling of that kiss fades away,
Slowly spinning into my surreality.

"Turning Leaves"

It seems like they're always falling,
Twisting, turning in the wind,
Like love's circuitous path
Looking for a comfortable haven,
A resting place.

Colors of Fall are Nature's beauty;
Red and orange, those shades of passion
Replace the coolness of green
As temperatures fall.
So can the heat of love
If we allow feelings to temper.

As leaves collide with the ground
Some stick to the dampness,
Like love hitting a wall
With nowhere to go
When hearts don't coincide.

But as those leaves decay
They add strength to the soil.
So it can be with our mistakes
That we might learn and use
The gift we've been given.
All may not be lost
Even with an early frost.

Turning leaves can teach a lesson;
Love takes not an easy path,
Both good and bad can happen.
But as a tree retains its strength through Winter
We too can survive the cold.
Like Nature patiently waiting for Spring
Love's warmth can be right around the corner.

"Only One Wish"

If memories were thoughts easily buried
Then I'd have no problem
When the thought of you
Crosses my mind.
If you hadn't smiled that day
I would have never said hello.
If I had never held you in my arms
I would have no desire to hold you again.
If I had not traced the lines of your face
I'd have no need to feel that kind of beauty
One more time.
If I had never touched your mouth with mine
I would have never learned
How meaningful a kiss can be.
If I had missed that chance
To make love to you
Then what I'm feeling now
Would be nothing more than a wistful memory.

If I had convinced you to stay
There would be no need
For the thoughts I'm having today.
If I had been the kind of man
I should have been
We would have never said goodbye,
The way we did and when.
If I had only one wish
It would be to have all those beautiful moments
Return to me.
That would mean
You would be right here
To forever stay.

"My One Temptation"

Head and shoulders above the rest,
The one I can't resist;
If you came calling now
I'd find a reason
To see you somehow.
Can't fully explain the attraction,
But deep inside burns that fire
Which won't die down.

It's purely physical and that's okay;
Temptation of the flesh,
A most powerful force,
Matter over mind in the strictest sense.
When it came to sin
You were always my source,
And I've readily admitted
The trouble I was in.

I have said all the words
In futile defense of your honor
And your integrity;
They have fallen on deaf ears,
Those who do not believe.
My wish is to find you okay,
And that your detractors
Have nothing left to say.

You are my Dulcinea,
The woman of my dreams,
And I your Don Quixote,
Flailing at windmills along the way,
Searching endlessly for a sign
To aid my impossible quest.
This is what you've done to me.
Your burning memory allows no rest.

"The Back Row First"

All bright and shiny, appearing almost new,
All dressed up for you,
But buyer beware;
Some have hidden mileage,
Defects not easily seen;
Looking older under closer inspection,
Their signals can flash false direction.

Front row models are there for good reason.
You'll stop to admire their lines and curves,
But under their hoods, inside their engines
Is the true test
Separating the clunkers from the best.

Yes, they have lots of options,
Some even worth a second look.
But don't always go by the Blue Book,
Because dollars don't always make sense.

Look behind those sparkling facades,
Check the back row first.
They might look a little duller,
Somewhat out of date,
But you just might find
Your reliable driving mate.

You can't always tell a book by its cover;
Sometimes plainer could be the greatest lover.
Take her for a drive if you dare.
See which key turns her on,
But buyer still beware;
No matter what price you pay
Love carries no warranty.

"In Her Lover's Eyes"

Any song she likes
Becomes his favorite one.
Anything she says
Is like music to his ears.
When he gets too high
She brings him back
To where he belongs.
When he's scared
She calms his fears.
When he's down and blue
She makes him feel
Unfettered and free.
When he worries about other guys
And possible infidelity
She puts him at ease.
For him she's everything she can be,
A lover and a friend
He can tell anything to.
She can do no wrong.
In his eyes
She's the only one.

"Smiling Back"

The old man crumbles to the floor
Before the last forced breath,
Before the finality of death.
His memories nearly broken by his side,
But he gathers strength and enough pride
To pick them up,
To remember.

His head floods with water colored visions
As he tries to remember
His life in better days;
Of what he was, what he used to be.
But he's weakening, barely holding on
As he thinks about them
And murmurs those old songs.

The names start coming back,
The pretty faces shining through,
Eyes brown, green, and sky blue.
Some won, some lost,
All part of the game.

Barely hearing the knock on the door
He starts to smile, but still on the floor,
For now he's remembering them all.
He's gone his very last mile,
And they notice despite his eyes being closed
He's wearing that happy smile.

"Undying Flame"

It matters not who you are
Or where you've been,
You may have a lot of money
Or looking down at your last ten.
We all have that fire,
The burning desire to be with one another
In the most physical way.

We've all had our Juliet,
Or perhaps our Helen of Troy.
There is always one,
Somebody we couldn't stop thinking of.
Some like to say it's chemistry,
That overpowering physical attraction.
But the only equation that makes sense,
The only numbers that really matter
Are one to one.

When that certain someone draws near
One can actually feel the warmth,
That fire burning.
Even the slightest blush
Might give it all away.
Don't worry, it's all okay;
It means the feeling is real,
And it's never wrong to enjoy
That flame which burns in all of us,
Forever.

"Dreamer"

You called me a dreamer,
And I guess it's true.
It's not a bad way to be
When my dreams always involve you.

I can see us together soon
Even though we just met.
Any other woman makes little sense
To a man whose mind is already set.

You make me smile all the time,
It feels so right,
But I have a brand new problem;
The smiles come hard
When you're out of sight.

Lonely is not the word
I want to hear,
Not the word
I want to say.
You can change all that;
Be mine forever on our special day.

So call me a dreamer if you must,
Tell me I don't make sense,
But my dreams have us together
In present and future tense.

"It Will Never Be Okay"

Every moment we spent together
Returns to life
As I read those words
I wrote about you
For what feels like
So many years ago.

Your image is forever etched
In my memory;
No matter what I do
Or what I have to say,
In my mind
Your absence will never be okay.

Each and every dream
I will ever have
Will fall far short of your reality.
They will be a poor remedy
In trying to repair those lonely spaces,
My unwelcome partners for so long.

As I continue down this deserted highway,
And my life dwindles down
I often think of you,
The girl I could never put a finger on.
If memories could be like clouds
They would slowly drift away and disappear.
But those are thoughts I've never deciphered
As being concise or clear.

You have caused problems to be sure,
Sleepless nights by the score.
But on my stone
I want to be remembered
As the man who chased a dream,
The girl who seemed to be a ghost,
The person he recalled
As that special one.

"The Edge Of My Mind"

I remember how you said hello,
And the way your foot
Happened to bump into mine;
You got my attention for sure.
All that stuff and more
Softened a man
Sadly stuck in the blue.

That night has been etched in my memory;
It has stayed with me forever.
It only took that short time
To know you,
And you almost walked away with my heart.
You were different than the others
I had known,
Something I could see right away.

I've memorized the kiss
When you didn't have to,
And those words
You really didn't need to say.
You listened when others
Could have cared less.
You gave me attention
When I needed someone to be there.

The thought of you never quite leaves me,
Almost as if you have a reservation.
You've always been inside
And always will be.
I can't see myself ever escaping
Nor do I want to.

My hope is that we'll always be friends,
Maybe someday more but never less.
If we listen to our hearts
We might learn all we need to know.
If not be rest assured
You will be with me forever,
On the edge of my mind.

"A Letter For Lauralei"

Dear Lauralei,
I'm sitting here thinking of what to write,
What to say
To make you understand
Why I have to be leaving today.
I must admit your Daddy was right,
But he didn't know
It would happen this way.

On this bus writing this letter,
Rain coming down,
Typical leaving weather.
Now looking back,
Thinking of you and me,
Realizing our love could never be.

That love came so fast.
I often wondered how long it would last.
We tried to be secret but people talk,
And now I'm taking the longest walk.
I'm almost 68 and you're only 24.
What exactly were we hoping for?

When you said you loved me
It really made no sense;
A young girl like you should have been
Somewhere in my past tense.
My love for you no surprise,
You'd be the ideal in any man's eyes.

I couldn't give you the long goodbye.
Seeing you cry would have been too much
Or listen to you ask for a second try.
It's better if I go to another place.

Don't cry for me now
For I'll be with family and friends,
The best of company save one.
But there is one thing I'm leaving behind;
It's my heart, but it pleases me to know
It will be in the best of hands.

Oh, there's this something I never told you,
Because I said I'd never lie;
I've been sick, and I'm leaving to die.
But I wanted to say it one last time;
I'll always love you, my sweet Lauralei.

"If Dreams Could Only Come True"

I saw you again last night
Looking more beautiful than ever,
Only in my dreams but so real
As if you were actually here,
Not some vague transparency.
Again it made me realize
I can never leave
The thought of loving you.

I've become your prisoner,
An emotional captive to a memory;
From the imaginary chains that bind me
I can never break free;
They hold me fast,
Still clinging to a love
That could never last.

As surely as life returns every day
Thoughts of you
Never escape my mind.
I've tried pills of every shape and color,
Red, green, yellow, and blue,
But none fit the bill,
Make me forget
There's only one script I need
And that would be you.

Only a fool believes in miracles,
Something he cannot see;
Then call me a fool
For still believing in you.
I've been so lost and lonely,
And no one else will do.

It feels like so many years
Since I last held you tight,
And I had relinquished hope.
But my phone rang last night;
That number looked so familiar.
Maybe miracles can happen,
And some dreams do come true.

"First And Last"

The night was still and damp
Like the back of your neck
As my fingers crossed right to left.
A response was felt,
And I held you for a secret moment
Daring to think of we.
As I touched your mouth with mine
I was swept away to a long time ago
When love could be so new,
And then I tasted you.
It had been so long
Since I had felt that way,
And I kissed you again;
I drank my fill
Hoping the tingling would never end.
It felt as if my tongue
Had reached your soul.
But there in the shadows
He was watching.
As I drove away I knew
That the first would be the last
I would hold you so.

"My Private Heart"

If you're very quiet
You might hear it now;
There's still life there,
Faint but still beating.
Splendid isolation has been its home.
It's been broken so many times before,
Enough to take most to the floor.

It's been so long
Since a woman has graced my door.
I might not know how to act,
What to say, what to do.
Now into my life there is you.

You can be my heroine,
Rescue me from the romantic dead.
I'll need much more than a jump start
To prevent this dormant love life
From totally falling apart.
You can be the one to break the chains,
To release my feelings from the incarceration
They find themselves in.

Just thinking of you
Has returned my smile,
Something hiding in a closet overtime.
The moment has come to question myself
If it's what I want
Or better left without.
There's only one way to find out;
It's time to introduce you
To my private heart.

"In Another Life"

Someday we just might meet again,
And I'm keeping my fingers crossed
That it won't be forever
Until your Blues gaze upon mine.
We'll have a lot to do
To make up for lost present time.

Distance keeps us apart,
People seem to interfere,
And there's that generation gap.
Let's not fool ourselves
It's a lot to overcome,
But if two hearts are willing
We can have it all and then some.

In another life
Our wishes could come true,
Difficulties left lost in our past.
Once left for dead,
Our love would be so new,
And only the best of memories
From then and now
Would be the ones to forever last.

"This Life Without You"

Call me crazy
If it sounds right,
But rest assured
You're never far from my thoughts,
But way too far from sight.

I don't give a damn
What your fortune teller says.
There will come a time
When it all makes sense,
And you will finally understand
Where I'm coming from.

It almost feels like evil spirits
Are getting between us,
Forming an invisible wedge
Between two hearts;
Stopping us before we can even start.

I do remember
All the things I've done wrong,
And I'll never relent
'Til I make them right.
Oh, there's one thing more;
I'll never give you up
Without a fight.

Your long absence by sight and sound
Hard to swallow.
But our time will come
If we show understanding and patience;
Until then only sweet memories
Permit my heart to follow.

"Butterfly"

I can only guess where you've flown to;
Like a beautiful Butterfly flitting to and fro.
Your free spirited ways never allow you
To light for long in one stable place.
You haven't taken the time
To absorb your surroundings
Or taste the sweet nectar
Of what your life could be.

I can only carry my net so long
Hoping to catch you by surprise,
Because for quite some time
You've been number one in my eyes.
I can only hope and pray
That you will settle soon,
And leave behind those endless flirtations
For some other day.

Like the Butterfly your time is short,
And the years can take their toll;
Your colors will lose their lustre
Faster than you could know.
Maybe the time has come
To stop flying around,
And start standing on solid ground.
Take on accounting of where you are,
And I'll be patiently watching and waiting;
Your okay will not have to travel far.

"Pardon My Fantasy"

My kingdom for your hand,
My treasures for that smile.
With the passage of time
We'll get more comfortable
Like words coming together
To create perfect rhyme.

Pardon that fantasy of you and me,
Present in my mind
For quite some time now.
Did you think I would forget those nights
Your attention become salvation for me?

Misty dreams are sweet and nice,
But fall short of the real thing;
You in my arms and not disappearing
When the rising Sun wipes our sleepiness away.

You have become my Muse
As well as my imaginary lover;
I will not rest
Until fantasy merges with reality,
And you are able to understand
That your heart is a special one
I can't afford to lose.

"Port In Any Storm"

Take care my love,
For when you leave me now
There will be risky chances
As well as forbidden dances.
There will be strangers in your midst,
Not always the most welcome company,
And people are not always
What they seem to be.

I will cherish our moments,
And remember you always,
But safety is not your neighbor;
That thought always torments me.
For I know
What you have yet to discover;
That evil resides in some,
Dangers lurk,
And they will surely come.

So take care my love.
Remember me as a positive force,
One who might alter your ragged course
If allowed to re-enter your life,
But only if I am welcome,
And you show no remorse.

Give it a chance,
And lovers we can be.
I'll keep you safe and warm,
Shelter you from threatening storm,
Protect you from impending harm.
So choose with care my love,
And you might be able to see
That I just might be
Your final destiny.

"Love's Pirate"

Sailing through love's open ocean,
At times smooth, other times rough,
The Moon full on calm water,
Eyes open wide and flags flying,
Setting sight on guarded treasure,
The most valuable booty.

No maps to follow,
No certain scheme in mind,
Only following one's senses,
The most ardent kind.
If storms come with feeling
May they enter the fray;
One should expect it that way.
It can be tough sailing
Trying to chart the course.
Love's uncertain way
Can be swamped with remorse.

Still hoping for signs of land
Where endless seas meet sand.
Maybe she'll be standing there,
Perhaps within reach.
As a man steers his love life
Through ports unknown
At least one thing is a certainty;
Through love lost and found
He has grown.

"My Fancy Dancer"

What we want and can't have
Will drive us crazy
If we allow it to,
And I want you.

Circling a smoke filled stage
With so many moves,
Mirrors reflecting two of you.
Making my head spin 'round,
Forcing my mind out of control,
But lovin' every minute,
Wanting more, much more.

Man and woman connecting
In a sweaty moment
Moving in sync with one another,
That animal feel.
I don't want it to stop;
Let it go on and on.

I want to sweep you away,
Show you what I can really do,
Who I really am
If you only knew.
And what I'm feeling now
You would be with me,
Older man, younger woman,
Intriguing fantasy.

So dance the night away,
But save one for me,
Maybe two, maybe three;
We'll come together again
To create that last dance, that feeling.
If I have to wait all night
It's okay.
You're worth it any day,
My fancy dancer.

"l Need A Lover"

My nights seem so long,
The days endless too
As I realize once again
Just how lonely I am.
I don't know who you are
Or where you'll be;
You could be the girl next door
Or maybe miles away.

I need someone to share secrets,
And someone to make new ones too.
But it's one of the hardest things to do,
Finding someone to help me through.

I'd surrender all the riches I have
Just to share that easy feeling.
You might think me a dreamer,
And that I might be.
But a man without dreams
Can survive only so long
Before giving up on everything.

I'm afraid to be running out of time.
Help me get back where I belong.
There must be a better way.
This life is way too short
To feel this lonely so long.

You could be young,
Perhaps you are old,
But I need a lover, a friend as well.
What we say and do
Behind closed doors
We'll never tell.
Like an unfinished song,
An unwritten poem
Our story has yet to be told.

"No Less Bright"

As the Moth is drawn to the flame
My mind returns to visions of you.
Your face glowing by candlelight
In a place so dimly lit.
Everyone looked ghostly,
And perhaps you were only a dream.

Burning the candle at both ends,
Trying to recall that sweet love affair.
It's been so long
Since we've extinguished that wick;
Remembering all the details
Will be quite the trick.

I see a long-legged beauty,
The eyes of a Cat
With the graceful moves to match.
You were just too good;
There had to be a catch.

I thought I knew you well.
The smell of your skin
Graced with scent,
The taste of your mouth,
We had started to jell;
Whatever it was felt meant to be.

I awoke the next morning
Half out of my mind
For I had lost my dream lover,
Apparently the spectral kind.
No candle, no flame, nothing left to light,
And I was left wishing
That you would return;
If not, that dreamy memory of you
Remains no less bright.

"Like Magic"

What seemed like another lost evening,
Just a dead end street,
With no one new or exciting to meet
Changed so very fast
When you appeared.

Your presence ignited the room,
And it didn't take long to see
That I wanted you for only me.
It had been so very long
Since a woman had made me feel
Like I belonged.

With moves like a Ballerina,
So graceful to the eyes,
Every step you made
Was like a cool breeze,
Refreshing my senses
Which had gone stale,
Reminding me how good it's been
To be a man,

When you were center stage
It was like pure magic,
Your brilliance stole the show.
I couldn't help but stare.
The sight of you
Became my only view,
And as the minutes passed by
My desire to know you only grew.

The music stopped,
You finally stepped down.
When you spoke your name
I couldn't help but smile.
It sounded so beautiful and right,
And I knew I had found my star,
Shining bright.

"The Yearbook"

Every now and then
I turn to those pages
To read again and again
What you wrote.
I still remember how we were together,
Two young kids thinking of love,
Not knowing what it really meant.

A smile slowly crosses my face
As I think about our favorite song,
And the memories it brings back.
We had it all, you and I,
But it was so quickly gone
In the blink of an eye.

Hard to believe it's been fifty years or so.
I'll never forget the way you looked
For our special dance.
In some ways little has changed;
You still radiate that special glow.

Walking into that old familiar gym
All the faces seem foreign now,
Save for one.
You've still maintained
Your good looks somehow.
Maybe it's my imagination
Or a case of wishful thinking,
Hoping to bring back our past.

Reality can be harsh at times,
Not always what we want to see.
As I held your hand
For one last time
That exact thought surrounded me.

Our love lives in that book,
And that's where it should stay;
What we once had
We can never bring back.
So when I returned home
I read your sweet words once again,
Most likely,
For the very last time.

"The Same Old Songs"

No one could fully understand
The effect you had on me
During a time
When I fashioned thoughts
So far from reality;
I wanted you to be everything,
Wanted you to be the one,
My hope to take all the hurt away.

Today when I hear those songs
The memories start floating back;
It all feels so familiar to me,
How I used to drive for miles
With that music playing
To be with a girl
I just had to see.

I remember those nights
Like they were yesterday;
The first time I heard your name,
The words we spoke,
The things we did,
The feel of your skin,
The depth of your kiss,
My desire to take you away.

I remember the letters I sent,
The poems I wrote,
And how you loved them so.
I so wanted to be your hero,
To rescue you
From a dark and hopeless place.
But it was like chasing a ghost;
You were so quickly gone
While barely leaving a trace.

You disappeared from my life
As fast as you came.
I'll always wonder what could have been,
And I still see your face
When that music plays.
But that vision is now broken
As I try to recall
Who I was, who I used to be
In that distant time,
That distant place.

"Love Through Chemistry"

It's no great scientific conclusion.
Let's not live with that illusion.
It's always been and will forever be
Love through bodily chemistry.
Body to body, skin to skin,
What happens during a clutch
Has to have that human touch.

You've heard of love at first sight,
But that's not always right;
It's more to do with first contact,
That physical commitment,
Like an unspoken contract.

We usually know from the first kiss
Whether it's a hit or miss;
We sense disappointment or bliss.
If it's the latter send along a sturdy ladder
Along with a little H_2O,
Because you'll have a runaway fire
Complete with afterglow.

No scientist can predict the elements
Which produce this sexual attraction;
Lovers don't even know.
Suffice it to say
It's a man and woman combination
When there are seeds to sow.

At times these lab sessions
Produce man and wife
While others are just for fun,
Maybe only once and done.
But when there's heat there's fire,
The kind of combustion
Of which we never tire.

It's a different type of science
On which we can have no reliance,
No set formula, no certain result;
It's simply a survival of the hottest.

"Unlikely Lady"

I saw you through rose colored glasses,
Always in the brightest of lights.
As others shunned you,
Tossed you aside
I saw only the best,
Perhaps with blinded eye;
Maybe I was telling myself
A most comfortable lie.

As disparate as two lovers could ever be,
But we had our night of magic,
And it passed so quickly by
Like Comets falling fast
Through the nighttime sky.

Now I cling to what I remember most,
The beauty you brought to me,
The way you made me smile,
Warm moments we kissed;
Those are the very best
Which I've sorely missed.

If there is justice in this muddled world,
And that's doubtful at best
You'll remember me
As the one who stood by you
While others would not.
And maybe you will return
To finally take my hand
When you have learned
Who you really are.

If you arrive too late
Make a promise to keep:
That you will stand by me,
Not leave me alone
As I rest forever
In my field of stone.

"Where The Heart May Go"

Much has been written,
And it's been oft discussed,
The heart and mind together
Or separate,
Which one rules,
Whether or not they can work in unison
Or do they best function apart?

I don't pretend to have all the answers,
So confusing the feelings at times;
They befuddle the mind
With too many options,
Too many ifs, ands, or buts.
You could always say
That in any given circumstance
Maybe one should listen to both.

One might make common sense
While the other is ruled by emotion,
One may say stop
While the other says go.
Perhaps a meeting in the middle
Might be the answer
One needs to know.

So tough to plot the course,
So hard to foretell the future,
But remember this for sure:
Well laid plans often go astray;
At times they can be changed
By what the heart has to say.

The heart causes emotions
The head might never consider.
It puts words in our voices
Sounding so beautiful,
Those which the mind might never summon
Or give us the courage to say.

The heart will notice things
The mind might never visualize;
What's right before our eyes
Can be seen in a wholly different light.
If we could only readjust our sight
To focus on what makes us smile
Here and now,
To not outthink ourselves,
To rely instead on what's inside,
And where the heart may go.

"Love's Suicide"

Pretty faces come and go,
But one always seems to hold him so;
She appeared to be his answer,
The final solution
With all her beauty, all her charm.
But alongside beauty
Can also come harm.

A woman can cause a man
To do the strangest things,
To lose his direction,
To lose his focus on what is proper.
And danger can exist
When attraction begets addiction,
And the heart causes the mind to wander.

She's like the Spider
And he the Fly;
The web she spins holds him tight.
No longer can he choose
Between wrong and right.
He is helpless to escape
And wonders why.

Looks can be deceiving,
Intentions even more so;
The closer he looks
She starts to lose her original glow.
Too late he begins to sadly realize
That instead of giving
She's much more into receiving.

Chasing unrequited love
Is like hurtling through Outer Space
Totally out of control
With no landing spot in mind,
The turbulence ending with a crash;
It's like committing love's suicide.

"100 Years"

Once in a lifetime
You might see that face,
That gentle smile,
That approving nod,
Freckles caressing those pretty cheeks.
But never in 100 years
Will another come my way;
I know that now,
But I don't know how
I'll make another day.

The feeling is still there,
But there's nothing but air.
Only the walls see my silent stare,
The floors feel my careless feet,
Not sure what turn
To take from here.

That bed feels like on ocean
Flooded with emotion
As my tears are its covers
Where once laid
Two most unlikely lovers.

100 years from now
No one will know who we were,
And no one will care,
But we had our time;
That's all one can ask,
A chance to be together,
Maybe just for a day,
Perhaps an hour or two
Out of 100 years.